Chaos and Dancing Stars

Jean Katz

BOMBSHELTER PRESS / LOS ANGELES

2002

Bombshelter Press
http://www.bombshelterpress.com
books@bombshelterpress.com
PO Box 481266 Bicentennial Station
Los Angeles, California 90048 USA

ISBN: 0-941017-66-4

Printed in the United States of America
Layout & Design: Alan Berman

Cover illustration: *dancing star '82;* serigraph by Corita Kent,
1982. Reprinted with permission from the Corita Art
Center, Immaculate Heart Community, Los Angeles.
Back cover photograph by Itzik Moskovitz.

For Norman,

who sustained me through the chaos,

and drew me toward the stars.

Contents

Where Poems Go

Thank you for your poems.
I used them for some of my interviews.
Best regards, Jim.

I stare at the penmanship.
A year ago I sat next to Jim
at a retirement luncheon.
We chatted about life, writing, creativity.
He said, *I write, too.*
He asked me to send him some poems.
Several weeks later he sent a thank-you note.
Now, a year later, he writes that
he took my poems with him
into the juvenile jails,
into the bare rooms,
each with a table and two chairs,
a tape recorder,
fluorescent light tubes overhead,
where he interviewed ten children
who had committed murder.
He opened my poems,
read one or two at random
to each child.
Afterwards, one of the girls, age 13,
who had murdered her boyfriend,
began writing,
sending poems to him.

I reread his note,
carry it to my bookshelf,
lay it on a side table,
pull out my folder of poems,
and examine the pages
under a bright light.

Radio

Once, only radio brought me the world,
On Sunday nights I listened
to Jack Benny and Fred Allen.
On weekdays I'd listen to
my Dad's early morning show
as he played country music for the farmers,
inviting them to come
buy bargains from his store.
His Polish-Yiddish accent
and 1930s country music.
"Dat vas Henk Villiams, und now kahms
Spike Jones und de City Slickers."

What fun to play on the radio waves!
What fun to have your say
with no back talk!
Laughter and honor and customers coming.
"Yager's moofed ahp tsu bring prices dahn.
Vork shirts cost only tree dollahs dis veek."
The cash register clicked and clanged
louder than the chatter of customers
buying their socks.
The second story store with bargains galore.
The merchant showman,
microphone in hand,
making you smile.

The Iowa farmers must have chuckled
to hear that Polish-Yiddish-English wit
while they shaved and ate their pancakes
before milking the cows
and planting the corn.

The Whole Trial

I'm always way too fat.
When I was a kid
the worst was being fat
and hearing the other kids laugh at me.
Dad accused Mom of overfeeding me.
He said so in the courtroom
while I sat outside
on the stone bench,
looking at the floor tiles,
hearing their voices through the door.
I sat there during the whole trial,
two or three days, maybe.
He said he wanted me.
She said she wanted me.
That judge was no King Solomon.
He split me between them.

Mom stayed in bed
from January through March.
"The flu," she said,
"I can't get over it."
When I came home from school
I sang and danced for her.
I tried so hard to make her smile.
I really wanted to run away,
to ride my bike
back to school so I could
jump rope and play hopscotch,
sit with the other kids
on the cement
playing marbles and jacks.

That time still gnaws inside my stomach
and still makes me want to eat.

Knowing the Name

No one knows his name
until the last breath goes out.
Rumi

I lust to name everything.
I'd like to skip across the street
to smell the purple bells,
really high on a bush.
What is their name?
There are purple brushes
like the ones we use to clean bottles,
and purple clumps
that grow without much water.
What is their name?
I know the purple blossoms,
bursting like fireworks,
are Agapanthus.
Lobelia is the tiny blossom
lining the edge of the garden.
I know the tree is a Jacaranda.
It hangs over my street,
dropping petals like lavender snowflakes
on the sidewalk and road.
I want to stick out my tongue
to catch them
but I'd better not.
Oleander blossoms are poisonous.

Lilacs grew in our garden in Iowa.
In Spring you could smell lilacs,
lilies of the valley and bridal-wreath.
First, purple and yellow crocuses
peeked above the snow.
Then yellow forsythia arched over.
As soon as the ground was dry

Mother took out her old bedspread
to lie on it, naked in the sun.
She said it soothed her, healed her,
made her melt into the earth.
She wanted me to lie with her,
but I wouldn't.
A neighbor man stood behind the
purple lilac bush, watching,
yet Mom didn't leave.
She continued to melt into the earth
where everything finds
its proper color and name.

My Twelfth Birthday Party

When the time comes for giving presents,
I walk to a little raised stage
with a microphone and a small table
where all the presents are piled up.
I look out at my girlfriends
sitting at restaurant tables.
I admire each package, untie the ribbons,
and slowly open the books, slips, blouses,
comb and mirror, scented talcum powder.
I say a big smiling "Thank you" after each present.
When all the presents have been opened
my father drags in a large heavy package,
too tall to be a bike, too bulky to be clothing.
I untie the bright red bow on top,
tear off the wrappings,
and find a bathroom scale,
the kind they have in doctors' offices.
I look at the weight lines, 10-20-30-40-50 . . . .
I look at my classmates
who are trying to suppress tittering laughs.
I look down at my body—
I see the fat belly, budding breasts,
thick arms and fingers.
I look back at the scale,
then at my overweight father,
and turn again to my guests.
I grit my teeth, smile, and say,
"Thank you for coming to the party.
Thank you for bringing me the nice presents."
I turn off the mike
As my father eats
the last frosting from his plate,
I walk off the stage and sit down.

Speaking the Light

God said, "There shall be light,"
and light came into existence.
Genesis 1:1

When I was little my grandpa
spoke the day into being.
I woke to the scent of coffee
from the kitchen,
and the smell of slaughtered chickens
from the butcher shop next door.
The smell of blood mixed
with the smell of dirt and singed feathers.
The sky was dark, but I could hear
Grandpa chanting the Hebrew morning prayers—
Modeh ani l'fanekha. . .
His voice was louder than
the chickens squawking outside.
With each chant more light
came into the room,
until I could see him through my bedroom door,
wrapped in a white prayer shawl.
Leather tefillin came down
from a wooden box on his forehead
to wind, first across the back of his neck,
and then around his arms.
On his head, a small black satin skull-cap.
In his hands, the prayer book.
He stood and swayed as he prayed
before the Eastern wall of our flat,
facing the gas station next door,
facing Milwaukee and Jerusalem,
facing the rising sun.
"Grandpa, why do you do this?
What is it?" I asked.
"Teach me what you do."
"This is not for girls," he said.

7

Now I, a grandmother,
stand wrapped in a prayer shawl,
in the synagogue,
swaying, chanting my grandfather's prayers,
bringing on the Sabbath day
as the morning light grows.

Back on Track

Yellow buttercups grow at my feet
as I stand at the side of the highway,
waiting for a tow truck to pull
the rented car
out of a ditch.
I had caught sight of a deer.
Norm stopped, backed up the car
so we could get a better view.
The left wheels slid into the ditch.
The tow-truck finally arrives.
It maneuvers around the car.
The driver, in blue overalls and red baseball cap,
walks all around our car,
bends over, and peers underneath,
hooks a chain from the truck
to its underside,
then climbs back in the cab.
Slow pulls get the car back on the road.
The car shakes and shudders
as it rolls back to flat ground.

That shaking reminds me of the time,
in a writing class,
when my life seemed
to have fallen off its track.
An image came to mind
of my bedroom in Wisconsin,
the narrow bed, the rumpled sheets,
the scent of freshly slaughtered poultry
from the butcher shop next door,
Mother sharing my bed,
nightly embracing 12-year-old me.
I saw my dumb acquiescence.
I thought that was

the way life had to be
now that my parents were divorced.

The teacher watched me write.
I shook and shuddered like our car,
getting back on the flat surface of the road.
She said, "Jean, are you all right?"
"I will be," I answered
as I staggered out the door.

Grandpa's Rocker

The thrift shop man just carried Grandpa's rocking chair out of the garage and put it on his truck. It is the chair that Grandpa sat on, at the top of the stairs to our flat, where he read the Yiddish newspaper. Sometimes he turned to look out the window at the traffic on Main Street in Fond du Lac, Wisconsin. He looked down to his left at the gasoline station where cars stopped for gas and directions. Then he continued reading. The fumes from that station were a permanent odor in the flat, along with the scent of newly slaughtered chickens from the meat market next door. The liquor store downstairs did not send up an odor.

That chair had curved arms that were worn from the sweat of Grandpa's hands, slats on the back where he rested his shoulders after dragging home a wagon full of overripe fruit for Grandma to trim and can. It had a wooden slat on the top where his head rested, when his eyes got tired from reading. He sat there at sunset every day, a round black skullcap on his head, davening the end-of-day Mincha prayers, bending forward and back with the rhythm of each blessing.

Some evenings he pulled the chair into the living room to read to Grandma while she rested on the couch. He read the advice-to-the-lovelorn column from the Yiddish paper. First he read the question. Then he and Grandma debated what advice they would give before he read the answer. It was the best communication I ever saw between them. Most of the time she nagged him to do things. He remained silent, resisting.

I have dragged that chair all over the United States since he died, forty years ago, thinking that one day I would refinish it and use it, but I never did. When the new buyer sands it down to the original wood, the wood of the farmer-craftsman who made it, she'll find Grandpa's sweat deep in the grain, the soft sound of his davening echoing with the creaks as she rocks.

Tante Soreh

Tante Soreh was so tall, her gray hair pulled back in a tight, no-nonsense bun, her solid frame, always wrapped in a clean white apron. It was to her house that we walked every Saturday afternoon, Grandma, Mother, and I, down Main Street, the Main Street of Maureen Daley's *Seventeenth Summer.*

We entered the house through her little sundry store where people picked up their kosher meat and rye bread on Thursday. Here they exchanged the gossip of the tiny Jewish community of a farm town in Wisconsin. We came on Saturday to hear the gossip. Grandpa had already picked up the meat and bread in his child's red wagon. Tante Soreh's house smelled of fresh-baked challah, kugel, cake, and kuchen. It smelled like a really good bakery .

Tante Soreh was the strong one of Grandma's sisters. She had a different fire. When she couldn't agree with her mother, she picked up, unmarried, and left her little village near Minsk for Odessa. There she supported herself making hats. She left Odessa for Paris, learned the bakers' and caterers' trades, and met her husband. Together they came to America, to Fond du Lac, Wisconsin.

Soon her husband died. She started the store to support herself and three small children. She also cooked and baked for all the town weddings.

Lately my aunts have told me Tante Soreh had had a lover for 15 years. They say that he took advantage of her good cooking and earning ability, then up and married someone else, moved into the new wife's house a few blocks away. Why didn't they tell me sooner? It might have made all the difference. They all kept me chaste as a nun, ignoring the stirrings inside. "Only date Jewish boys," Mother said. There weren't any.

"Never have sex until marriage," she said.

"Don't go to parties. The food will make you sick."

"Don't leave home. You need Mother to protect you from men and milk."

Mother believed that she and I and most of the world were allergic to milk. I wasn't.

When I left home for college. I met men and drank milk. Still the velvet covered chains bound me. If I had known about Tante Soreh and her lover those chains might have been cut a whole lot sooner.

Mi Ken Neit Essen Bloomen

When I was 12
I worked in the garden with Grandma.
It was in a vacant lot a block away
from our cold-water flat
above the liquor store,
next door to the gas station.
We pulled weeds between
the green beans and cabbage,
staked up the hard green tomatoes,
sprinkled carrot seeds
in the freshly dug furrows.
I wanted to plant some flowers.
"Bobo," I asked, "far vas farflaunst du
  nisht kein bloomen in dem garten?"
  (Grandma, why don't you plant
  some flowers in the garden?)
"Mi ken neit essen bloomen."
  She reached for a tiny tomato plant,
  dug a hole, dropped it in,
  mounded the earth around the root,
  patted it down.
  That was her answer to everything:
"We can't eat flowers."

Once she told me
how her mother raged
at Grandma's sister, Tante Sarah,
when Sarah embroidered
colorful flowers on a handkerchief.
Great Grandmother threw
the embroidery into the fire,
screaming, "Mi ken neit essen bloomen!"

I just brought in flowers.
A rose for the kitchen table
placed in a crystal vase
between sugar and honey.
African violets go
to the window ledge.
A paleonopsis orchid
in the living room,
slow to open, long in bloom.

Azey. Azey.

Grandma rarely spoke English. She sat on the couch when Grandpa read to her from the Yiddish newspaper. She stood by the stove, stirring the soup, or bent over the garden, pulling the weeds, or she scrubbed the clothes on the glass and wood scrub board. She slept in flour-sack nightgowns that she had sewed herself. The nice, lace-trimmed nightgowns that her daughters gave her were saved in a drawer, in case she would ever have to go to the hospital. She never went to the hospital.

There was a treadle sewing machine in her bedroom. She sewed all the clothes for her three daughters and nieces and nephews on that machine. After Mother and I moved into Grandma's house I wanted to learn to sew. I sat beside her in her bedroom, begging her to teach me. One day she took my foot and placed it on the treadle. Then she sat beside me, arms around my arms, hands above my hands. Her arms felt warm. She smelled like Ponds soap. She showed me how to guide the fabric as the needle moved up and down, making a seam coming toward me, while my foot pumped the treadle. Her hands guided mine to turn a corner, pinch the puffs, lay tiny pleats, stop, tear the thread, and start again. I pushed the cloth through. "Azey," she said. "Azey." I don't think she said a word beyond "Azey. Azey." (Like this. Like this.) My eyes and hands and body learned to sew.

Thirty years later I taught my 12-year-old daughter to sew. She was so impatient, face pinched, body tight, crying in frustration. She said, "Tell me how so I can do it. I want to do it myself." All I could say was "Azey. Azey."

My husband's dad taught me how to drive the car when I was 20. He sat beside me in his car as I drove along Wisconsin country roads, my hands tight on the wheel. We passed fields of corn and pastures filled with cows. Sam watched the road without saying a word. He raised his arm and gestured for a turn to the right, or a move to the left, gestured to speed up, slow down. Finally I parked the car in front of his house, took a deep breath, sighed, handed him the keys, opened the car door, stepped out, and walked into the house.

When my daughter was 16 she took drivers' training in school. She begged me to practice with her. I sat beside her in our car as she turned from Beverly Glen onto Wilshire Boulevard at rush hour. Cars hurled at us from all directions. My teeth locked together. I couldn't find the words to tell her when and where to maneuver to maintain her course, change lanes, slow, straighten the wheels. All I could say was "Azey. Azey." Suddenly I made her stop in the middle of traffic. "Get out and change sides, Lisa. I'll drive. You'll practice with Dad later. I will ruin you as a driver if I practice with you. I can't find the words fast enough." We passed each other walking in front of the car. She took a deep breath, sighed, handed me the keys, opened the passenger door, and got in.

Bread and Violets

After the big Los Angeles earthquake in 1994 the Los Angeles Times carried a story about a woman who planted flowers along her fence near the street as soon as the rubble was cleared away. When the reporter asked her why she was doing that so soon after the quake, when there was still so much work to be done, she answered, "My mother always taught me, 'If you have two pennies to spend, spend one on bread and one on violets.'"

Bread and violets. That woman could have been my Aunt Anna.

I'll bet that when people in Escanaba, Michigan reminisce on their front porches they talk about that pretty Jewish woman who moved away to Texas around 1970. They remember how she lived in a house by a scrap metal yard, but always had beautiful African violets and philodendron in her house. Outdoors, as soon as the snow melted, there were forsythias, crocuses, lilies of the valley, tulips, lilacs, peonies, hydrangeas, violets, and roses, surrounding a fish pond in the middle. She was a rose herself, always wearing bright red and blue dresses, matching necklaces and earrings, and polished leather pumps, as she bargained with the fur trappers and scrap metal collectors. She wore a gold and turquoise brooch on her jacket when she climbed onto the boxcar at the railroad station to make sure no one cheated her on the weight and quality of the scrap steel she was buying. She used to tell about coming to America at the age of four. What she remembered best was the blue color of the Atlantic Ocean.

A story my Grandma Bella, Aunt Anna's mother, told me was about Grandma Bella's sister, Tante Soreh. When Tante Soreh was a young teenage girl she embroidered pretty flowers on a handkerchief. Her mother raged at her, threw the embroidery into the fire, shouting, "Mi ken neit essen bloomen" (We can't eat flowers).

Aunt Anna must have heard that message often in the dirt floor wooden cottage of her infant life in the Russian village, in her childhood house in Fond du Lac, Wisconsin, where her father left every morning in his horse-drawn wagon to peddle junk to the farmers. At night he piled the metals he had bought into the back yard. The message rang in her ears when she was a young widow running a scrap metal business and raising two sons in northern Michigan during the Great Depression. Again she had scrap metal in her back yard. She never let the family message, *We can't eat flowers,* stop her from making sure that in her house, along with home-baked challa, cakes, and pies, there were plenty of roses and plenty of violets.

Tamed

What does a nice Jewish girl
from Iowa know about wild?
My wild cannot seep out
of any crack or crevice.
Not when Mother watches
my every breath, bite,
and trip to the bathroom
until I am 18.
Not when we share the same bed
until I leave for the University of Wisconsin.
I have no dates,
no parties, no beer or wine,
no food that isn't kosher
at friends' houses or restaurants.

Young elephants are tamed
by attaching their legs
to each other with a strong chain
so they can only take small steps.
Later they can be controlled
by a thin bracelet.
That is how I am tamed.
Attention is the chain,
constant, unwavering attention.

When I start dating in college
passion starts up.
I sit in the front seat
of my boyfriend's car,
just kissing for hours.
He goes back
to the fraternity house
with my lipstick all over his face.
He tells them we did more.

The fraternity boys come over
to my sorority house
to serenade me.

The night I turn 21
college friends celebrate my birthday.
They slice the top
off a huge watermelon,
mix the pulp with gin,
poke many holes in the top,
then place 21 candles on it.
They sing.
I blow out the candles.
We put straws in the holes,
sing and sip until the straws
draw only gurgles of air.
I sip only a little.

Years later, in Madrid,
I watch a matador
in gorgeous satin and braid.
He has tamed his own wildness
to a perfect discipline and graceful art.
He watches the wild in the bull
with the same unwavering attention
that Mother trained on me.
He stands still,
waits for the bull to move forward,
and, at the precise moment
when the bull makes his move.
comes in for the kill.

Wild spirit, my gift,
like beauty and love,
is over-tamed.
I am the docile school girl,
hiding her gifts.

Good Girl

Mother had told me about sex,
the pain,
the demands,
the duty,
the messy wetness,
the babies,
never the beauty,
the sweet warmth,
the passion.
When I got ready to marry
I went to the doctor for a check-up.
He put me on the scale,
measured my height and weight,
took my blood pressure,
drew some blood from my arm.
He told me, "The hymen
should be broken before marriage.
Then the beginning of marriage
won't be so painful."
I did what I was told.
I walked from our flat on Main Street
past the drunks in front of the tavern,
past the county courthouse, bank,
department store, and Montrose Hotel,
up the stairs into the red brick hospital.
Mother walked beside me.
Her face had a long, worried expression.
A nurse took us to a small bare room
with a standard examining table.
The doctor told Mother to wait outside.
I lay down on the table,
put my feet up in the cold stirrups.
I spread my knees wide,
showing my private place

to a stranger for the first time.
The nurse stood beside the doctor
as he broke the hymen
with a small sharp instrument.
The nurse helped me to sit up.
She gave me a pad
to wear in case of bleeding.
I walked home with Mother,
a good girl,
ready for marriage.

Rosie Picus

I first met Rosie Picus in 1952. Norm and I had been dating for about three months. "Let's go to my sister's house," he said. "She's having a Chanukah party. Her husband, Harry, makes great latkes." I had watched my grandma make potato pancakes every year. The recipe is pretty simple, but everyone's got their secret method. I was scared about meeting Norm's extended family, but eager to go. We weren't engaged, or even thinking about getting married.

I walked into the room full of strangers, everyone talking and gesturing at once. Norm's sister, Ethel, was putting bowls of apple sauce, sour cream, meat balls, and salad on a buffet table. Harry was frying latkes in the kitchen, then tossing them onto paper towels before he put them on cookie trays in the oven. I'd never seen it done that way. I had met Norm's parents, Bessie and Sam, once or twice before. They were sitting on a couch, talking Yiddish to a tiny older woman whose gray hair was pulled back in a tight bun.

"Jean, this is my grandma, Rosie Picus. Grandma, this is Jean," Norm said. Grandma looked me over, nodded, but didn't say a word. She turned to Bessie and Sam and lamented, "Vas is das? Norman nemt a shiksa?" They were wondering why Norm was dating a non-Jewish girl. I admit, I didn't look very Jewish with my almost blond page-boy hairdo, saddle shoes, bobby socks, and straight, narrow nose. They continued whispering in Yiddish, but I could hear them perfectly well. "Oy vey is meir," they said. "Es vet zien a shandeh." Intermarriage was considered a bigger sin than murder, adultery, or driving on the Sabbath.

Not only was I Jewish, but unlike Norm's sisters and most of the girls of my generation, I could understand and speak fluent Yiddish. Having lived with my Yiddish speaking grandparents from age 12 to 18, I was quite adept at the language of my ancestors.

I leaned toward them and whispered in Norm's grandma's ear, "Bobo, Ich been a Yiddishe shiksa" (Grandma, I'm a Jewish shiksa). Her eyes grew very wide. She looked me over again from head to foot. "Shaina Maedel," she said as she moved over to sit beside me. Now she had someone else to talk to besides her daughter and son-in-law.

She told me about her life in Russia and about her husband, Norm's grandfather, Ephraim Katz, who was a scholar and teacher. He didn't have time to earn money. He spent his days in the study-house, poring over the Torah and Talmud, and prepared a few boys for their Bar Mitzvah. It fell to Rosie to make a living for the family, while she raised Max, Bessie, Sam, Nathan, and Yetta.

She did what many wives of scholars did in those days. She ran a roadside tavern. The Russian soldiers and peasant farmers came into her tavern to drink vodka after work.

Rosie stood up to tell me the rest of her story. She threw her hands back over her shoulders as she said, "Ven de soldaten habn sich shiker gevoren, Ich hab ze aroisgevorfen vie fliegen, aroisgevarfen vie fliegen" (When the soldiers got too drunk, I threw them out like flies, threw them out like flies).

Marriage

Marriage:
an alignment of two souls,
spirits, bodies,
like jigsaw puzzle parts,
fitting perfectly in and out of each other
at some edges,
with other edges that don't align at all
for private space.
Like two spoons nested
together in a drawer,
or the master craftsman's cabinets
that needed no nails,
the parts aligned so tight
into a perfect fit.

The breathing is in rhythm,
like the matching steps
on the morning walk along the shore,
or the dance steps
to the favorite tune.
It is eating from the same pot
and spending from the same pocket,
complementary talents,
not identical.

Friendship is the glue,
when glue is needed,
when small and major earthquakes
rock the alignment.
Best friends
who see each other
through the pains,
past the strains,
over the rocks,

round the blocks,
who listen more than talk,
read each other's eyes,
resonate to each other's tones.

Warm passion, too,
and trust,
and laughter,
and silence,
and playful silly hours,
and love, beyond description,
love.

A Different Poem

One arm is flung
across my waist.
The other rests
on my thigh.
I'm awake,
press my back
into his soft, warm
chest and stomach,
our thighs entangle
as we breathe in unison,
the sleepy rhythm of the morning,
a stirring in my loins,
my morning fire.

I remember how the babies,
sucking at my breast,
awakened that same stirring.
I'd put the babes to sleep
and wait until his fire came.

Now, again, I have to wait
for the familiar caress,
the sensuous touch,
the rediscovery of
our own rhythms:
timing, peaking, sighing,
as we return to
sweet, easy breathing.

Why do they call it fucking?
Harsh word for sweet coupling,
blood and flesh, breath and fire.

Years ago I sat beside a man
I was beginning to love.

His arm rested
on my shoulders.
His voice was amorous.
"I want to fuck you," he said.
I had wanted to make love with him.

If he had wanted to make love with me,
or I had wanted to fuck him,
this would be a different poem.

Out of Reach

I don't want to grow old
the way my mother did.
I can see her the day I drove
to Wisconsin to get her out of jail.
The jail was clean and new.
She was the only woman prisoner.
The attendant met me at the entrance,
took me by the elbow,
guided me to Mother's cell,
explained that Mother's downstairs neighbors
called the police about water
leaking through the ceiling.
When they went up to investigate
they found her naked and chanting.
All of her possessions were
heaped in the living room,
water overflowed the bathtub,
soaked through the floor,
and leaked into the store downstairs.
The police took her to jail
until they could find her next of kin
to put her in a hospital.

I looked through the steel bars
of the cell at the brown tile floor
and brown tile walls,
a cot in the room
and one light bulb
with a circular tin shade,
all so clean.
Mother wore a brown, dirty bathrobe.
It hung open to show
her pubic hair and sagging breasts.
Her ribs showed through her skin.

Her feet were in ragged, scuffed slippers.
She paced up and down,
chanting in her cell,
"6-7-8-9 5-4-3-2 12-13-14-15."
Her eyes flickered.
Perhaps she recognized me.

I put my hand through the bars
to close the front of her bathrobe.
She moved out of reach.
"Mama," I asked, "what happened?"
"7-8-9-10," she answered, "3-4-5-6."

Geraniums

In the '60s my husband and I
bought a fine old home
in a "changing neighborhood"
on the south side of Chicago.
Neighbors were young families like ours.
After lunch we mothers
would wash the dishes,
bathe our babies,
put them down for naps,
then phone each other
to organize a house and garden tour
to bring buyers to our neighborhood.
Geraniums were our symbol,
so bright and hopeful.
We invited the Governor,
who came and listened
when we told him
to stop the realtors
from redlining our area
as "Blacks only" or "Whites only,"
to give mortgages to all
who want to live here.
We took off our aprons
and went to see the mayor.
We didn't march with Dr. King in Selma;
we were busy working
for South Shore in Chicago.

We were so naïve then.
We didn't know Mayor Daley
would tear gas the students
who were protesting the Vietnam war
in Grant Park.
When he did

we put away the groceries,
put the kids in the back seats of our cars,
and drove to Michigan Avenue,
to march with the students.
Our children carried signs:
Stop the War.

We didn't know that apartment owners
would fill one-family apartments with two families.
We didn't know that street gangs
would bring their turf wars to our streets,
trampling the geraniums.
We didn't know that so many
old neighbors would move away.
We never would have guessed
that some new neighbors
would want us to move away,
or that we would.

Learning Sportsmanship

Little boys run
in every direction
across the field,
kicking a soccer ball.
Some follow the boy who kicks it next.
Others go after a leaf blowing,
or a butterfly,
or a dog that wandered onto the field.
They're five or six years old.
One team wears blue tee shirts
with numbers on the back,
black shorts,
blue socks pulled up over the calf,
and sneakers.
Other boys are dressed
in green and black.

Their fathers stand
at the side of the field.
"Kick it harder, Tommy."
"Billy, the goal is
the other way.
Turn around."
"Kyle, follow the ball
after you kick it."
"Tim, when the ball
comes to you, kick it."
"No, Billy, the other way."

Finally one father calls,
"Blue Team, come over here."
The ball lies on the grass.
The little boys run over to huddle
around the coach.

He points across the field
to the other team.
"Now remember, boys,
  first we assassinate them;
  then we appreciate them.
  Can you remember that?
  First we assassinate;
  then we appreciate.
  O.K?
  Now go out and win."

Death of a Salesman

When my dad returns home
after a long workday,
he wants a hug, a hot meal, a comfortable bed.
His second wife screams at him
about the leaking faucet,
that his son hasn't done his homework,
that his daughter doesn't smile right.
She allows him to sit on only two chairs in the house,
a kitchen chair for eating
and a La-Z-Boy recliner for watching TV.
He's not permitted to sit on the plastic covered
silk damask couches and chairs.
Lamp shades glow above porcelain stands
shaped like French courtesans.
Wide gilt frames surround small pictures of flowers.
No room here
for a man who trails cigar ashes,
drips gravy and watermelon juice on his vest,
earns the money,
pays the bills.
Like Willy Loman,
he has a great imagination.
He pretends that the salesmen and customers
who come to his store are his friends,
that his business is booming,
that his family is happy and successful.

Chicago Garbage

The painter's drop cloth
drapes the stairs
leading to our bedroom.
Every corner of the house
is filled to brimming:
a rack of clothes,
a pile of shoes,
a stack of books,
so the painters can work.
This house feels
like our house in Chicago
just before we moved.
The movers boxed everything
that wasn't nailed to the walls.
When we arrived in L.A.
I slashed the tape of each carton
with a razor.
A bad smell
rose from one box,
as if something had died there.
The movers had packed our garbage
and trucked it across
the Mojave to California,
a reminder that there is no such thing
as a clean start—
our garbage comes with us.

The Fall

My daughter sleeps, a hand under her cheek on the pillow, thick dark eyebrows, ringlets of dark brown curls above her forehead, the softest sound of breath, almost a snore. I've watched that face since she was born, almost 40 years ago. Now she waits for the call to adopt her baby girl. I think about her as a mother, about me as her mother, about my mother.

My mother never watched me sleep when I was 40. By then I was watching her, catching her when she fell ill and went mad. I wish I could bring Mom back to this room, to be with us, just to be, easy. It was never easy.

I remember a day when I knocked on Mother's door. There was no answer. I called, "Mom, Mom." No answer. I rattled the door. No answer. Reaching into my purse, I found my key, turned open the lock, turned the knob, pushed open the door, and walked into her apartment. It had a burnt potato smell. In the kitchen I turned off the stove and called, "Mom, Mom," again. No answer. When I walked into her bedroom I saw her lying on the floor, breathing softly, the rise and fall of shoulders with each breath, a little blood on the carpet where she lay. Touching her shoulder, I said, "Mom" in a soft voice.

She stirred, opened her eyes, sat up, and said, "Jeannie, why are you here?" I told her about the locked door, the burnt potato pan, the stove still lit.

"How did you fall, Mom? Why didn't you answer my call? Where did this blood come from?" I asked.

She said, "The rug slipped. I think I hurt my arm."
Her wrist and hand were turned and crooked, with a
red swelling at the joint.

"Does it hurt?" I asked as I touched it.

"Yes," she said.

"Mom, we have to go to the hospital to have a doctor
look at it."

"No! No hospital! No doctor!"

"Mom," I said, "We have to. It may be broken."

Somehow I guided her into my car and drove her to
the hospital emergency entrance. The attendant at the
the counter took down the information. He said, "We'll
get you set up for x-ray as soon as possible."

She screamed, "No! No x-ray! I won't!"

The attendant looked at me. He said, "Are you her
legal guardian?"

"No."

"You will have to take her home," he said. "We can't
touch her without her permission."

I drove her home, helped her out of the car, into her
apartment, into bed. I made sure the stove was turned
off. "I'll call you in the morning," I said. After driving
home, I parked my car in the garage, walked up the
stairs, into the house, found my journal between the
cookbooks, and sat down at the kitchen table to write
"Mother Says No to Everything."

Mother Says No to Everything

He's calling to you, Mother.
>*No.*
He'd love you, Mother.
>*No.*
He wants you to bear his baby, Mother.
He wants you to share his joy, Mother.
>*No.*
The baby is growing in you, Mother.
She wants life, Mother.
>*No.*
Will you give me milk, Mother?
Will you give me honey, Mother?
Can I trust this ground, Mother?
Can I trust this water, Mother?
>*No.*
I want to grow, Mother.
Will you let me go, Mother?
Will you sew my clothes, Mother?
Will you buy me pretty shoes, Mother?
>*No.*
Mother, life is calling. May I go?
Mother, there's a party. May I go?
Mother, there is good food. May I taste it?
Mother, there is college. May I go?
>*No.*
Mother, there's a man. May I marry?
Mother, he has fine parents. Come and meet them.
>*No.*
Mother, I have honors. Come applaud me.
>*No.*
Mother, I've a baby. Hold her.

Mother, I am weary. I need help.
Mother you are weary. May I help you?

       No.

Mother, I am forty and rejoicing. Come and share it.
Mother I am angry and can't bear it.

       No.

Mother, here's a gift. Will you take it?
You are sick. May I heal you?

       No.

Let me go.

       No.

Accept my care.

       No.

Let me go.
Will you die, Mother?
Will you live, Mother?

       No.

Your will is no, Mother Woe.
Will is woe, Mother, when it is no.
Woe is no, Mother Woe.
Woe, no, woe, no, no.
You cross your legs, Mother Woe.
You clench your fists, Mother No.
You grit your teeth, Mother Woe.
Nothing in, Mother No.
Nothing out, Mother No.
Let it go.
Let will go.
Let woe go.
Let *no* go.
Mother,
let me go.

Mother's Legacies

Mother wouldn't leave Chicago
until she found her tweezers.
She held it in the car all the way to Iowa.
Later she gripped it five hours
on the plane that took her to California.

Each year she grew more chin sprouts.
When she could no longer see,
she asked me to pull them,
then cried because she thought
pulling caused more to grow.
One day she said, "No more."
I couldn't change her mind.
People who lived at
her board and care house complained
when she grew an unkempt beard
like a Chinese mandarin.
When she had to be moved to convalescent care
the orderlies shaved her in the shower,
She cried and fought, begging,
"Jeannie, take me out. Don't let them force me.
They have no right."

Every morning I run my finger
along the line of my chin,
feeling for any stiff hair
that may have sprouted in the night.
When I find one,
I pluck it out with my silver tweezers.
These chin sprouts, my need for sequence,
this before that,
that after this,
and my ear for poetry,
these are my mother's legacies.

Gemini

Two of me
live inside my skin;

I do the laundry,
set the clock beside the bed,
make to-do lists,
know all the rules,
and what the rules are for;
say things right,
do things right,
and maintain the order
of ordinary days.

She dreams she's dancing,
scribbles poetry after midnight,
yearns for adventure,
and can destroy my order
with a blessed fantasy.
Her fire singes
the hem of my skirt,
but my lifetime of
living by the rules
keeps her flame in check.

A Matter of Morality

It is Saturday morning.
At the door of the
Hyatt Regency in Sacramento
I speak to the bell-man.
"I plan to walk
for an hour around here.
Is there any street
I should not walk on?
Is it safe?"
"No problem," he tells me.
I wear my red paisley dress,
black linen suit jacket,
silver butterfly pin,
nylon hose, and tennis shoes
with heavy cotton socks.
I walk out,
forgetting that I still wear
my convention name tag.
I walk around the capitol,
admiring the Roman architecture.
The camellias, azaleas,
and fruit trees blossom.
A wisteria vine is
dropping its violet petals.
The capitol shines in it's fresh paint.
A mural a block away
catches my eye.
Colorful, cartoon-like,
it shows the work of
the Civilian Conservation Corps.
I study the details.

A stocky woman walks toward me.
She has blond short curls,

a fair but ruddy complexion,
pink sweatshirt, faded blue jeans,
scuffed sneakers.
She walks with a man who looks
like a floppy, denim scarecrow.
They are talking loudly
about Jesus and God.
We get close.
She stares at my name tag.
"What's your name?" she asks
"Jean," I say.
"I'm attending a conference in Sacramento."
She punches me in the shoulder, hard,
and walks past me.
I turn as she goes by me,
and catch my breath.
"I wouldn't hit a stranger," I say.
"Yes," she says,
"It is a matter of morality, isn't it?
But I know you."
She continues walking
down the street with her friend,
talking, again, about God, Jesus,
and the Church.
I walk on, too, pain subsiding,
remembering the day they phoned me
from the convalescent hospital
where Mother was staying.
It was the day of Lisa's confirmation.
"Your mother got up in the middle of the night.
She walked into the next room.
She punched the patient in that room.
Then she started putting on
the other lady's clothes.
Come and get her.
You will have to take her someplace else.
We can't keep her here."

My mother weighed 85 pounds.
She could hardly see.
She wouldn't bathe.
She wanted me
to take her home, quit my job,
take care of her.
I considered taking her
to the crossroads
of the freeways at rush hour.

I attended Lisa's confirmation ceremony,
served cookies on a silver tray
at the reception.
I said, "Hi. How are you?"
I nodded my head.
I shook hands.
I put on fresh makeup.
I posed for a picture
near the alter with Lisa,
my arm around her shoulder.
The photographer said,
"Smile."
I smiled.

Visiting Dachau

The bunkers are lined with orderly rows of berths.
The order, itself, a demon's trick.
We visit the crematoria,
where my uncles' and cousins' bodies burned.

Birds sing here.
Flowers bloom.
Behind double rows of barbed wire and concrete
the living earth continues to give forth life.
I pick up some soil,
rub it on my hands,
study it.

We drive back to Munich,
to our glass and steel hotel.
We open the shiny door,
check for messages at the desk.
I look at the International Herald Tribune.
There was an SLA shooting in California.
I ride the steel elevator to our room,
go into the bathroom,
wash my hands,
and scrub my nails.

Zipper

I hold the worn leash as we walk our spaniel,
Zipper, to the vet.
Fourteen years ago I carried that ball of puppy fur
home from a different vet,
feeling the same sensation
as when I carried our infants
home from the hospital,
wondering if I would know what to do.

Now our spaniel has become an old dog.
He can't see well, bumps into things,
pees all over the house,
leaves brown, smelly piles
on the living room carpet.

Dan and I walk with him for three miles.
He likes this walk.
He can still do it.
The vet's office smells of dogs.
Dogs are barking.
Zipper sniffs them all.
The vet takes us right away.
We say we want to stay with Zipper.
Dan and I run our hands over Zipper's fur.
I stroke his head and moist nose.
As the vet inserts the silver needle
we feel his warm body go limp,
then stiff, under our hands.
We stroke Zipper one more time,
then walk the three miles home,
the empty leash in hand.

What Is Your Function, Lady?

I pull a form out of an envelope.
The top line reads,
"Describe your function."
It says, "On the next lines
describe what you do, please."
I look at the form, look away,
open my calendar book
with all the appointments,
look at the papers tossed away
in my waste basket,
look into my desk drawer,
pick up my pen and begin to write,

"On any day I may
  initiate, instigate, innovate,
  inquire, integrate or infiltrate,
  promote, prod, pry, prepare, project, proliferate,
  procrastinate, and sometimes prevaricate,
  direct, design, develop, delegate,
  disseminate, decry, and always drive,
  stir up, simmer down, spread around,
  suspend, submerge, and even sink,
  coordinate, communicate, consult, calculate, consider,
  confer, cooperate, cogitate, and occasionally conceal,
  advise, analyze, associate,
  agitate, and frequently aggravate,
  write, read, reason, research,
  wrestle, and sometimes ramble,
  listen, loosen, lighten,
  link, launch, and now lament
  the loss of time spent on trivial tasks."

When they feed that into their computer,
I wonder what it will do.

Will it show me
facilitating a group discussion,
or training teachers
to handle conflict resolution,
or bringing planners to consensus?
I put down my #2 pencil.
I fold the form,
put it in the envelope,
walk to the office mailbox,
watching the other people
and what they do.

Cooking Chicken Soup

I'm cooking chicken soup again,
chopping carrots,
slicing celery and onions,
peeling skin off the
chicken breasts and thighs,
covering the chicken with quarts of water,
sprinkling in salt and pepper,
adding parsley.

I wonder if cooking chicken soup
is a form of prayer?
I wonder why I feel this urgency
to cook all the almost forgotten flavors,
to fill the house with
the aroma of soup, kugels,
kneidlach, tsimmes and borscht?

The urgency doesn't connect
with real memories.
My childhood holidays
were not so special.
The same newspaper tablecloth
covered the table as on weekdays
to save on laundry.
Candles were lit
on the back of a cake pan
to save from polishing
the brass candlesticks.
Chicken soup was an everyday food.
Guests were never invited.

At work my desk is piled high with papers,
getting ready for a conference.
I should keep working.
But a voice shouts in my ear,

"Close it up! Go home!
  Prepare chicken soup and kneidlach,
  kugels and borscht, tsimmes and teiglach!
  Invite guests!"

  In the synagogue
  I carry on a silent argument
  with the God of broken promises,
"How can I pray to You who permitted
  the burning of Your children,
  their ashes scattered across
  the wheat and potato fields of Europe?

"You, who are called Father
  in my prayer book,
  were no father to my father's
  murdered brothers and sisters,
  no father to the children
  of Tereisen or Maalot.
  We should prosecute You
  in court for child abuse.
  I cannot pray in the words
  of this prayer book.
  Only in the melodies,
  only in the swaying, chanting community."

Connection is the core of my spirituality,
  connection with my known and unknown past,
  with the mysterious creative force,
  with some eternal and unifying source,
  evoked by the aroma of chicken soup.

Some voice, some spiritual voice,
  whispered to me all week,
  shouted at me all day,
"Cook chicken soup, Jean,
  kugels and kneidlach,
  tsimmes and borscht.
  Invite guests."

Out of Nothing

Annie Dillard wrote that
men grew out of mud.
Then the rains came,
and we all melted.
It seems to me that God believes in nothing.
God is the great Ein Sof, the Tao,
the mystery, the emptiness
out of which all creation grows.
So, when the dove flew out from the ark
and found an olive branch
after all the seeds had drowned,
he plucked it out of nothing,
out of the emptiness.

God pushes out new creations
that break off and make their own choices.
It would be so easy
for the world we live in now to break,
with pain to those we love.
Our capacity for ecstasy stays buried,
whispering, but never fulfilled,
because we cannot say "Yes"
when a voice calls to us, wants us.
We shake our heads, turn, and walk away.

In the early morning
the light increases in the sky
with every step I take.
The clouds change color:
deep purple to apricot to yellow
and then to white.
Sprinklers arch and spray.
Birds chirp, louder than the passing cars.
I pick up a green orange that has fallen

from a tree beside the sidewalk.
It is the size of a tennis ball.
A piece of the stem clings to it,
a white spot of bird dropping on one side.
The orange reminds me, again,
how everything first grows from mud,
and God—that urge—
just keeps pushing the mud
into different forms.

Know Your Own Plot of Earth

Once they burned the books in Berlin.
Now the television sets are
catching flame all over the planet,
sending us all outdoors to join in the dance.
We circle the community bonfire,
then snake up the mountainside,
now flowing red molten lava,
as the peak erupts with fiery signals
to gods and mortals alike:
a new order on this quaking earth,
where I wince in pain when my hip hurts
and my ankle chimes like a gong in a monastery.

Wendell Berry says,
"Know your own plot of earth";
I wonder if his great-grandparents
escaped from the potato famine in Ireland.
His people were not herded
from their homes in cattle cars,
gassed, their bodies burned in ovens.
They were not chained on slave ships,
taken to places they never dreamed,
to be sold, worked till they dropped,
their children sold away.
Now only tornadoes mock his sense of place,
when living rooms suddenly rest in tree branches
and the grandfather clock floats down
the Kentucky River with beavers riding atop.
The children who didn't make it to the storm cellar
are swirled up into the dark tornado,
turned and dropped
on a chicken coop in Nebraska,
calling, "Mama."

Where I Belong

I am in this very white room with fifteen people, taking a workshop called Multi-Cultural Education. I live in Los Angeles. I had better learn this. The young man in the middle says his name is Howard. He says he is southeast Asian, Philippino. His skin is light brown. Black curly hair. Thick glasses. Wide smile. He listens to each question, looks at the person talking. Then he looks at the carpet for a long time before he answers. I ask him later about the history of his name. He says his Jewish grandfather sailed to the Philippines, stayed, married a Philippino woman. He was raised Catholic.

He tells us to walk to the corner of the room that represents the way we think we communicate. He has pasted up a word in each corner; Hawk, Turtle, Tiger, Rabbit. We go where we think we belong, talk to the others who also go there. We talk a long time.

There are a lot more exercises.

It is a day and a half later.

He says again, Go to the corner where you think you belong. This time he has pasted up signs saying African-American, Euro-American, Asian-American, Hispanic-American. I go to the Euro-American corner. Where else? I talk to the others. Something feels very wrong. I don't belong here. Never did. I think about the massacres, York, the Inquisition, Chmelnitzi, the Pogroms, the Holocaust, the sign outside the South Shore Country Club till the 1950s: "No dogs or Jews allowed."

We're not through.

He tells us to line up. Now step down if you are a woman. Step back. Now step down if your parents didn't finish high school. Step back. Now step down if you are a Jew. Just two of us step out. In my head I am at the train station, in the box car, rolling to Poland, to the camp, to the oven, inhaling the gas.

What Matters

I go through the motions
of ordinary Tuesdays,
fold towels, run to the store
for milk and bread,
answer the phone calls
from chimney-sweeps.
But, then,
as I carry out the trash,
I catch my breath
at the sight of
a drop of water
on a spider's web,
how it beads up,
reflecting the sun's light,
and I call my friend
to tell her about it.
She tells me that
she saw a skunk
walk across her garden
with five babies trailing behind.
They disappeared under a hedge,
and she forgot to go change
the motor oil in her car.
"Those white stripes," she says.
"Those beautiful white stripes."

Remember Her

Remember her,
standing by the cracked wall
on the dirty street,
swaying to the rhythm of her madness
as her blind eyes saw only dim outlines
of the leering cars and lecherous drivers.
The dust blew across the purple varicosities
of her matchstick legs
below the buttocks, thin as a skeleton,
below the ribcage pushing through the skin.
The face was wispy bearded like a Mandarin,
no smile, no frown, just the incessant chant,
the mantra escaping past the lips,
past the brown decaying teeth,
into the air poisoned by fumes of diesel trucks
delivering toxins to the local grocer
where lead-deadened children stumble
for a daily fix of chips and juices
which have never seen a vitamin,
or milk from cows whose daily diet of DDT
contaminates even the milk
the woman could never cause to flow
from her sagging, stinking breasts.

She said the nurses pushed hard things
into her anus to punish her.
Suppositories to make her shit.
She didn't know. They couldn't say,
the foreign orderlies and nurses
who tied her hands
so she wouldn't smear feces on her face
as she chanted her Yiddish mantras,
Yiddish curses to the world that wouldn't nourish
in the rooms that smelled of the urine

of all the drug-placid grandmas
who had lost the power to charm
or wheedle favors from anyone.

Don't forget her,
peering through the lace curtains
at the cars on Main Street,
driving north to south, south to north,
while she raised herself on toes
and dropped, flat-footed, a hundred times in place,
as the dust pussies gathered
under the dining room table,
and the scent of cabbage cooking
mixed with the scents of slaughtered chickens
and gasoline to fuel the trucks
carrying the butchered bulls and calves
to distant markets,
as her arms turned like windmills in a storm,
warding off the demons of imagined disasters
symbolized by milk,
the poison mothers pass on to infants
straining at the dry, cracked breasts
as empty and hollow as the spirit,
crushed by daily words of rasping, cackling rejection
you wouldn't notice unless you tuned in that station
on the wireless where the hate of Father Caughlin
mixed with the gas that came from Nazi showers.

The rectangular hole in the ground
was just the right size
for the shriveled woman in the plain pine box.
Only the eyebrows retained their bushy life.
The teeth had cracked and rotted.
Most of the flesh had long since abandoned
the brittle bones under the sagging skin.
At last the eyes were closed.
A lace insert covered the shriveled breasts
inside the white shroud

where she waited to be lowered
into the fresh-dug hole under the olive tree
on the hill overlooking the freeway
where cars perpetually moved
north to south, south to north,
as they had below her window on Main Street
where she had walked every day,
turning back if she saw a broken bottle
or a squirrel or a ladder casting a shadow,
an omen that her venture was unwise,
was cursed with tragic outcomes.
Better to hide behind those curtains
and wait for better omens
as the cars passed north to south, south to north
under the curtains that were a shield
to ward off all the dangers
of the evil eyes and evil spirits
that would enter if she didn't chant enough,
didn't rise and fall on toes enough,
didn't hide enough,
didn't measure drops of milk
from an eyedropper onto sugar lumps
to inoculate her daughter
against the dangers.

Before the End

Orderlies you don't know
sit on your bed,
smoke cigarettes,
speak languages you don't understand.
You matter no more to them
than the bedpans they empty.
They laugh, gesture,
tell stories about the women
they were with last night.
They won't leave.
Finally your daughter walks in.
Then, sheepish,
they snuff out their cigarettes
and move on
to push the next wheelchair,
empty the next bedpan,
serve the next meal.

Brown Shoes

A price sticker clings to
brown shoes in Mother's closet.
I bought them for her years ago.
Mother wore cracked, scuffed shoes
with holes gaping in the soles.
They were so dilapidated
they caused her to fall down.
One day I talked her into
going to the shoe store.
The clerk let her try on
as many pairs as she wanted
until she found a pair of plain brown oxfords
that looked just like the old ones.
She never wore them.

"If I wear them, they'll get worn out
  just like these," she said.
"I want to save them till these are really worn out.
  I want to save them till I get well."
She shuffled along every day in those old shoes.
Whenever I visited,
  she'd ask me to hide the new ones in a different place
so no one would steal them.
She worried about them all the time.
Then she got pneumonia,
  a fall, a fracture, then recovery.
She was supposed to practice walking,
  but she wouldn't.
"Jeannie, where are my shoes?" she'd say.
"Don't let anyone steal them."
"Do you want to wear them, Mom?" I asked.
"No, not till I get well," she answered.

At Mt. Sinai Cemetery,
under an olive tree,
grass covers the casket
with her barefoot, shrouded body.
In the closet the new brown shoes
in their wrapping paper
are still waiting.

Written in memory of Sarah Kohler Yager,
born January 15, 1904, Minsk, Russia;
deceased January 25, 1989, Los Angeles, California

I Wanted to Believe Anne Frank

I am the blue-eyed, brown-haired daughter
of Jewish immigrants who settled in Iowa.
I am the daughter
of the reclusive madwoman of Main Street
and the flamboyant merchant of the radio waves.
When I was 10 years old
my father heard the news;
they had burned his mother
and 10 sisters and brothers in Poland.
They had lined up his cousins in the Ukraine,
then shot them into mass graves.
Daddy and Mommy were getting a divorce.
I didn't know what to think about any of that.
Then, when I was 20, I read Anne Frank's *Diary.*
Before they took her away
she wrote, "In spite of everything,
I still believe that people
are basically good at heart."
I wanted to believe that, so I did.

Now, in my 61st year,
I listen to the news on National Public Radio
as I drive to work.
I hear about the Muslim mother in Bosnia
who taught her children to respect
and get along with everyone.
She wept as she watched her daughter
raped by Serbian soldiers.
Nine months later she helped her daughter
give birth to a baby .
"One day," she says, "I will teach
this boy to kill his father."
I hear about the Armenian daughter
who hid as the Azerbeijani soldiers

threw her aged mother out the window.
The reporter tells about
the Cambodian sister who had to stand quiet
as the Khmer Rouge soldiers
made her cousin tighten a wire
around her brother's throat
until his head fell off.
A Korean woman remembers the day
she was taken to be a "comfort woman"
for the Japanese soldiers,
forty men a night.
A reporter describes the Guatemalan woman
whose tongue was cut out for political protest.
A concentration camp survivor describes
Dr. Mengele using her and her twin sister
for surgical experiments in Auschwitz
when she was a child.
An Israeli mother tells her story:
Her child and 90 classmates,
studying at their desks,
were shot by Arabs
who invaded their school in Maalot.
An Arab bride reports that
her husband was taken from her side
on their wedding night by Israeli soldiers.
He was sent to freeze
in the snowy mountains near Lebanon.
They suspected that he was a Hamas terrorist.
A reporter interviews an African-American woman
in South Central Los Angeles
whose house was fire-bombed
when she publicly protested
the drug-dealing on her block.
Now the radio tells
about a gray-haired woman
who stayed in Compton
long after her white neighbors moved away.

"Why move," she said.
"The new neighbors are just people, too."
  As she sat paying her bills
  and figuring her taxes
  a neighbor youth with a gun
  took 12 dollars and her life.

I can't see the road through my tears.
My hands shake on the wheel,
  my feet tremble on the gas pedal.
I pull off the freeway
  near the path to Vasquez Rocks,
  turn off the radio,
  get out of the car,
  slam and lock the door.
If I had Anne Frank's *Diary* with me now,
I'd climb to the highest rock,
  tear the pages out, one by one,
  toss them, and watch the wind
  carry them into the desert.

Freedom Wheels

I'm not yet riding on wheelchair wheels.
I've spent 62 years
on carriage wheels, tricycle wheels,
bicycle wheels, automobile wheels.
My bicycle took me away.

When I was a child
I never imagined leaving Iowa
for Wisconsin, then Georgia,
Illinois, Ohio, California.
I never imagined that someday
I would pedal my own toddler
on a kiddie seat on the back of my bike
across Ohio country roads,
or that I would be biking by the ocean
on my 40TH wedding anniversary.

In Iowa I rode past
fields of corn and mounds of hay.
Now I pedal my bike along the Pacific,
the glint of sunlight on the water,
sun on my back,
wind in my face,
and always
the fear of falling.

A Life on Wheels

Afternoon in L.A. A peaceful Sunday. The fountain in my garden sings, masking a little the sound of the street down the hill, the steady roar where traffic never stops. Here a person can walk for miles, greet strangers' eyes, nod, smile faintly, and no one will stop her, ask her business, offer harm or help.

A few blocks away dark men gather at corners, scan the passing cars, watch for a signal to come on for a day's work. Down another street a playground where kids swing on monkey bars, slide down a red slide, climb up again, as dads push the swing, giving moms a break, or taking their day of custody.

In this town a woman just past sixty could drive forever in her old maroon Toyota, spotted white where the birds dropped their waste, scratched where other cars in lots have opened their doors. A sound in the motor worries her. She could live all day in that car and who would care. She could pick up an Egg McMuffun in a styrofoam box through a window for breakfast, park in the shade to eat it, carry her Starbucks covered mug of coffee, sip as she steers back to the road.

She listens to Derek Jacobi read the *Iliad* as she drives 80 miles to work, works a while, then drives up to the Jack-in-the-Box talking machine to order chicken fajita pita for lunch. A dark-haired waitress in a white dress and paper hat passes the fajita in a paper sack through the window, says "Have a nice day," puts the green bills in the cash register and gives her two quarters. The woman tucks a towel under her chin before she eats and drives again. More Derek Jacobi and the Pacific until she stops at the 7-11. The Indian man looks up from his newspaper when she asks for fat-free pretzels and a Diet Pepsi. A TV monitor overhead mirrors her moves in the store. She offers him two bills. He gives her change, says "Have a nice day." and looks down again at his paper. She remembers to ask, "Do you have a public bathroom I could use?" He hands her the key. When she is through with the bathroom she drops the key on the counter.

She could stop at an ocean turnoff, watch the Pacific, gulls wheeling, take out her kitchen timer, set it, and take a nap until it is time to go to her poetry class, or she could drive on further, past the coral trees on San Vicente, pretzels crunching in her teeth to keep her awake, listening to Homer describe the Trojan War battles.

Waiting Room

We strangers sit.
Knit.
Fret.
We chat.
Write.
Read.
We stare.
Pace.
Eat.
We compare.

Surgeons in green pajamas
pad in and out,
their feet clad in paper wrappers.
But, like the angel of death,
or the angel of life,
they crook a finger and draw us near.
It's touch and go, they say.
He's critical.
We're doing everything we can.
Or they say,
I'm sorry.
Or,
He's fine.
He lives.

I wait my turn
for my own green messenger
to appear in his paper booties,
bearing my husband's good
or terrible news.

What Is a Life Worth?

I am sitting in a small hospital room,
holding Norm's hand. The light is dim.
He spent the night on this bed
with all its monitors and charts.
I have returned, after sleeping at home,
to stay with him until he enters the surgery room.
He is half-dazed from some pre-surgery anesthetic.
Nurses come in, agitated.
They forgot to shave his body the night before.
They turn on the lights,
spread shaving lotion all over his hairy chest,
belly, around the testicles, and down his hairy legs.
They shave until his body glistens
like a baby after a bath.
What else have they forgotten?
They dry him, wrap him in warm blankets,
tell him the doctor has arrived.
Surgery will begin at 6:30.
He dozes and wakes again while I hold his hand.
We talk a little about whom to call
when the surgery is over.
At 6:25 I walk down the corridor,
holding his hand, as an orderly pushes his bed.
An intravenous feeding bottle hangs over him,
attached by a tube to his arm.
I kiss him at the door, wish him luck,
tell him I'll see him in a couple of hours,
and walk into the waiting room,
wondering if that was our last kiss.
I have made a decision.
I will never again sit in a toxic waiting room
with all the nervous relatives of other patients,
weeping, pacing, building each other's anxiety.
I find the exit. Outside the hospital

I head for the ocean to walk with my thoughts
until it is time to return in six hours.
I pass homeless men on the grass, some sleeping,
some drinking wine from bottles
covered with paper sacks.
A homeless woman pushes her shopping cart past me.
It is filled with plastic bags.
I think about how we are spending $70,000
to save the life of one sweet man.
We throw others away on the street.
I walk on, picturing my life as a widow.
That may be my story by noon.
I imagine hearing the worst news,
then feel guilty for my thoughts.
Some people think positive thoughts
may pull him through.
I picture the cold, empty place on his side of the bed.
I feel the emptiness of no embrace.
I hear the silence of no laughter in my kitchen.
I think of Norm's puppy-playfulness,
and wonder if I will forget how to play.
I remember all I still don't know
about money management,
which he does so well, and vow, again, to learn.
My arthritic thumb is throbbing.
How will I open jars? I pray as I walk,
every prayer I can remember from childhood,
pray that he recovers,
pray that I have the strength
to handle whatever happens.

My legs are really tired
by the time I find a restaurant on Montana.
I order an omelette with tomatoes on the side,
read the morning newspaper, retaining nothing.
I walk back to the hospital,
picturing my father in his coffin in Detroit, 1968.

He was so cold when I kissed him.
The undertakers had put on too much makeup.
I had persuaded his wife to get a plain pine box,
not to waste money on a fancy coffin
to go underground the next day.
Will Norm look like that tomorrow?
He always resembled my dad.

Returning to the hospital,
I ride the elevator up to the chapel to read the Tao
and Steven Mitchell's book of sacred literature.
I don't know how to pray.
A Mass is going on, too cheerful for my mood.
I hear responsive reading, like in the synagogue.
I notice the nuns are all wearing street clothes.
There is a modern sculpture of Mary.
At noon I ride down the elevator
to the surgery waiting room to meet the surgeon.
He appears in five minutes
wearing his green surgery pajamas,
paper slippers and hat.
He says, "Norm came through fine. He should be O.K.
You can go in to see him, but don't be frightened.
Stay just a few minutes."
I walk into the intensive care room.
Norm's skin is gray. His eyes are closed.
Tubes are in his nose, mouth, arms.
A long row of black stitches
tracks down his chest and thigh. I touch his hand.
He squeezes back, opens his eyes, and gestures,
as though asking, "How are you?"
I smile and say, "Relieved.
I'll call the kids. Get some sleep.
I'll see you tonight.
I love you."

Life Study

The nurse tells me to sit in the waiting room.
She has to prepare my husband for the angiogram,
maybe angioplasty for the sixth time.
I kiss him at the door of the catheter lab,
walk down the long corridor to the waiting room.
The dawn sun lights the buildings outside,
blinding me as I look at the window.
I won't stay here.

I have been memorizing Norm,
every pore and ridge: soft belly, hard ribs,
the soapy scent of him after a shower and shave.
A shower can change how he feels about anything.
He believes in showers as some men believe in God.
If I were Picasso I would draw Norm all in triangles,
his nose, the lift at the top of his lips,
even his eyes, the point at the top of each brow
and the two points beside the cleft of his chin.
No, triangles won't work.
His ears are pure curve, wider on top,
a small upward curve at the bottom.
And his hair, what is left of it,
still curls up at the back of his neck.
I comb and caress all the curls
of his body hair with my fingers.

Nine months ago I stood in a hospital emergency room,
watched the green line of Norm's heart monitor
swing up and down, erratic,
then stop, then start with a blip,
then stop, then start again with a spike.
The nurse pulled me into the waiting room.
When I checked the door, it was locked
so I couldn't return to the emergency room.

She returned five minutes later to say,
"He's alive now.
He gave us quite a scare.
You can see him in a half-hour."

This time I go for a walk,
remembering the triangles of his face,
the feel of the hair on his chest,
wondering how to make sense
of the green pattern on the monitor,
wondering what the doctor will say
when I get back.

Pick-A-Part

At the Pick-A-Part lot
dead cars are lined up in rows
by make and age.
People cannibalize them
to replace the worn-out parts of their own cars.
On the right side of the lot
they have opened a new division
where cadavers are neatly arranged
by age, gender, and ethnic origin.
They are pickled in some cosmic juice
to keep the organs working after brain death.
Signs state the age and cause of death
and parts already taken.

I'm searching for a woman, fortyish,
who still has
a sturdy miniscus for her knee
and a supple low back disc
in her spine.
There she is, near the fence.
They've only taken out a kidney.
No problem.
I don't need one yet.

I pluck out a miniscus and a disc
with a very large tweezer,
then some teeth, and, just in case,
an extra miniscus and two spare discs
for the next ones to go.
I unscrew two feet
for the replacements I will need soon.
Her feet have no bunions, no hammer toes,
no neuromas like pebbles between the bones.

I twist off two thumb joints
to replace my arthritic ones.

I drop them in my rolling wire shopping cart
along with the axle and door lock buttons
I picked up for my Toyota.
The check-out man tells me
there's a special on hearts.
I consider getting one for Norm,
but decide to bring him
with me another time.
He can get his own.

Gratitude

Adonai melech, adonai malach,
adonai yimloch, leolam voed.

As I walk my morning miles
I chant familiar Hebrew prayers,
inhale the scent of star jasmine,
the just-blooming gardenia
by the front steps,
and the fresh cut grass
of the golf course.
The wind blows cool on my face.
Just as I reach the corner
the first ray of sun hits my cheek.
It is warm.
There is the call and response
of the unseen birds.
A carpet of fallen petals is
under the violet jacaranda tree.
I see the lavender, star-bursting agapantha,
the soft curving pink, white, and yellow roses,
sweet white breath of ageratum at their base,
surprising orange poppies and ranunculus
where I thought they had faded months ago,
yellow trumpet lilies,
red, pink, and orange hibiscus
sticking out their pincushion tongues,
giant red and blue snowball hydrangeas,
a hummingbird sipping from a fuchsia
on its arched branch, yellow bell abutolon,
red and orange bougainvillea,
white clumps of azaleas, blooming since March,
pink and white oleanders outside my door,
shiny, deep green leaves and full,
waxy, white flowers of magnolias,

round yellow sunflowers.
Bright red, pink and white profusion
of geraniums, petunias,
impatiens, and waxy begonias
line the walks and flower beds.
Here and there are the yellow,
blue and purple pansies,
yellow and orange marigolds
surrounded by intense blue lobelia,
a neighbor's pale purple lantana hedge.

As I walk on feet that always hurt
this beauty carries me forward along the sidewalk,
up the next hill, around the corner.
My knee no longer hurts.
No sciatica pain radiates now
from the spine to the ankle.
My arms swing free.
With each breath I smell the fragrance.
With each step I count a blessing.
With each flower I chant the name;
Jacaranda, agapantha, lobelia, bougainvillea.
Gratitude: this Tuesday, this moment, my body,
this place, my husband, this solitude, my life.

What Was that Line?

She got up in the morning
with a phrase beating in her head.
It came at the end of a dream.
It almost faded as she ate breakfast
but she held on,
saying it under her breath,
planning to turn it into a poem
as soon as she had tidied up.
Then she noticed the list—
six phone calls before 9:30.
Of course, she made every one.
Sometimes she talked to a message machine.
Some calls led to more calls,
and notes on her To Do list.
She sat down at her desk,
noticed a drooping plant,
went for the water,
dropped seven drops of liquid fertilizer
into every quart,
walked all around the house,
pouring fertilizer water into the plants
till they were standing up again.
Back at the desk, she pulled out her poetry journal,
found her favorite blue ceramic pen,
and noticed a bill that was due,
She wrote the check to pay the bill,
and a couple more, due in a week.
The phone rang.
It was a call about a possible job.
She was to fax a résumé by afternoon.
At last she opened her poetry journal
to a clean page.
What was that line?
She thought she had better make lunch.

Maybe the line would return
when she took her walk.
What can I say about a woman
who chooses to make phone calls,
pay bills, water plants, write resumes,
while her poems wander off like stray cats,
unfed, ungroomed, not even petted.
She doesn't deserve to get poems. Not her.
If she ever gets more poems,
the cats should piss all over them.

Glacier Bay

I turn the calendar to February.
A puffin picture greets me,
red beak, white face, black feathers,
bright red and black eye,
the funniest creature,
popping in and out
of the water.
I laugh out loud
remembering them in Glacier Bay.
Not at all like the steaming pile
of fresh green bear scat
I stepped in on the trail
while I walked alone
in the mossy new forest
where the glaciers
had receded just 200 years ago,
leaving fresh sweet ground
for the bears to roam,
and me, awe struck,
oblivious to the danger.

Wooden Spoon

When my aunt was a little girl
she often refused to eat,
so her mother, my grandma,
stood behind her,
ready to hit her
with a wooden spoon
unless she cleaned her plate.
For the rest of her 96 years
my aunt's stomach tightened up
whenever she looked at a plate of food.
Sometimes she couldn't swallow.
When her 91-year-old sister eats,
she gets stomach cramps.
My mother, gone ten years now,
thought most foods
would make her sick,
especially milk, which she
always had to finish.

I took that wooden spoon
from Grandma's kitchen
after she died.
I use it in the morning to make oatmeal.
I put 2 inches of water
in the bottom of the double boiler,
put it on the stove on high.
Then I spray the top of the double boiler
with vegetable spray.
I measure in ½-cup long-cooking oatmeal,
⅓-cup dry powdered nonfat milk,
and 1 cup of water,
and stir it once with
Grandma's wooden spoon.
As soon as the bottom water boils,

I move the pot to a very low flame,
make coffee, get dressed,
and take a three-mile walk.

When I get back
the oatmeal is steaming
in the double boiler.
I stir it again
and whack the wooden spoon
against the pan.
The texture is creamy, firm,
and there are no lumps.

Grandma Is Watching

randma Beylya used a treadle sewing machine. She bent over it, pumping the treadle with her foot as she guided the flour sacks under the needle to turn them into night gowns. It was the only machine I ever saw her use.

I imagine her riding on my shoulder all day, today, like a tiny Tom Thumb, whispering in my ear, commenting on all the machines I use and the routines I follow. Her white hair is pulled back in a bun. Her shapely legs are lined with purple varicose veins like mine. She wears her old floral green house-dress.

Everything I do surprises her. First thing in the morning I take a pill to prevent my bones from growing brittle. Then I push the buttons on my kitchen timer to remind me to eat no other food for 30 minutes. Meanwhile I pack an ounce of dry cereal, a banana, and two ounces of hard cheese into a plastic bag to eat while I drive one hour to my first appointment. I pour decaffeinated coffee into a small thermos and put the breakfast supplies by the front door so I won't forget them.

"What is that?" Grandma asks. "What is it for?" She sees me turn on my computer to check my e-mail messages, and to type a few replies.

Driving to my first appointment I listen to an audio tape of an actor reading Will Durant's *History of Civilization*. I stop the car at an electrical supply store to buy a toner cartridge for my printer.

Grandma shrieks "Watch out" when I look over both shoulders, turn the wheel hard, and back my Toyota into a tight parking space while three lanes of cars speed past me. After I park I pulled my cellular phone out of my purse to call a friend who is recovering from heart surgery. Then I get out, slam the car door, lock it, and put 25 cents into the parking meter. "Do you have to pay to park on the street?" she asks. "Grandpa never paid to hitch the wagon."

Across the street is the travel doctor's office building. As I enter a door it opens automatically when I pass an electric eye. I push the elevator button. The door opens. I step in, push another button, and ride up three levels to the doctor's office. The doctor, a much younger woman than I, asks me about where I plan to travel. "Greece," I tell her. "Good," she says. "There is no cholera there."

Grandma whispers, "Thank God! Your mother had cholera when she was a baby. Maybe that is why she was always so scared of everything. Why do you want to go to Europe anyway? I came from there. It was no good."

The doctor gives me a hepatitis-A shot in the arm. Grandma says, "Why are you letting her shoot sickness into you? Didn't I teach you never to put a healthy head into a sick bed." "Don't worry, Grandma," I say. "This is to prevent sickness."

My last stop is a grocery. There I buy a large cut-up chicken, a bunch of carrots, two onions, celery, garlic, and a small plastic bag containing fresh dill. Finally Grandma relaxes. Now we are in the familiar world of food. When I pay $1.98 for the dill, she nearly falls off my shoulder, then shouts at me, "Can't you grow it in your garden? I never paid that much for a whole chicken." I stop at the bakery to buy challa for Sabbath dinner. "Don't you make it yourself?" she marvels. "I

saw that you have my kneading bowl in your cup-
board."

On the way home I drive through six lanes of traffic.
She tells me how she came all the way from Minsk, Rus-
sia to Wisconsin by train, boat, and train again. "I was
scared every minute," she says. "Your Momma was so
sick. I was so weak, always nauseated from the rocking
boat and the bad smells. Little Anna complained the
whole time."

When I return home my granddaughter, Miriam, is
waiting. She gives me a big hug. She can't see my
Grandma Beylya. I wonder if Miriam's life will be as dif-
ferent from mine as mine is from my Grandma's.

Appetite

The kitchen table is still
the symbol of my ambivalence.
Temptations tantalize the palate
after long days of abstinence.

I'm dieting again.
The years of trying and failing
are eclipsed by the myth
that only a slender woman is worthy.

The promise of ideal proportions
conflicts with instinct and appetites.
I watch this body expand and contract
like consciousness itself,
or a perfect souffle.

Lemon bars and M&Ms,
almond fudge ice cream
and omelettes with cheese
pale as the moon.

I say we burn all the diet books
in a bonfire as brilliant as cherries flambé
and eat and drink to our hearts' content,
till we crave no more,
and all that's left is to wait
as the juices digest
and the pulse shrugs and yawns
and hunger sleeps its forgetful sleep.

Riches and Silence

In absence is the beginning of desire.
Aviva Zornberg

Norm is traveling.
Spanish guitar music plays on the stereo.
A pile of letters are stamped,
ready to go.
I carry them eight blocks
to drop in a mailbox,
watch the sky turn mauve.
A green moon rises,
larger, brighter, nearer to earth
than it has been for 130 years.
It draws closer to me,
the craters so plain that
it's hard to leave the moon,
but I walk back home to sort paper
until the desk looks clean.
I turn on the television,
watch it for a few minutes,
then turn it off.
The house is not silent.
I hear the tick of the clock,
the scratch of my pen,
and the little squeak of the springs
when I fall onto the empty bed.

Sun and Shadow

All we hear is the sound
of pine needles underfoot.
Norm reads the hiking guide
out loud as we walk,
as if for my benefit.
"Mountain lions have been
sighted on this trail.
When hungry they attack hikers."
He pauses, waits for my response.
I keep walking.
Thistles bloom above spiky leaves.
A cloud of monarchs
flutters up from the flowers.
They ascend, then descend to hang
like tiny orange and black flags
from the thistle petals.
I pull out my camera.
"Don't you think we'd better
turn around?" Norm asks.
A branch snaps as a squirrel leaps
from a strong limb to a broken one.
I turn, afraid I might see
yellow fur in the distance.
Another branch snaps.
"We'd better go." Norm says.
I take one last picture
of the butterflies,
step back, then turn
and walk as fast as I can
through the shadows
to the trail head,
leaving the monarchs
to flutter again.

Path to the Ruins

We dock at the port of Aegis, the pistachio capital of Greece. The late afternoon sun makes every whitewashed wall glow orange. Down the wobbly gangplank we walk into a town, like the others, lined with gift shops and cafes, trinket stands and roaming vendors. We talk about what to do until dinner. Norm wants to shop and I want to take the path to the ruins of the Temple of Apollo, but I also want to please, so I join him for a block, holding hands. The trinkets are the same as in the last port. Even the t-shirts are the same. I keep looking over my shoulder toward the Temple. Finally I say, "Norm, this isn't for me. I'll meet you back at the boat at 6:30."

It's often like that. He wants to go one way. I want to go another, but I also want to do what he wants, so I go along for a while. Then something in my chest constricts. I have to go my own way in order to breathe.

Norm buys a bag of pistachios, and gives me half to put in my pocket. "Be careful," he warns me. "Remember the time in Naples, when that man tried to touch you in the museum every time you went through a narrow door. And the time in Rome when a man chased you through the park after you asked him for directions."

"I'll be O.K.," I say, and walk toward the Temple, down the oceanside trail, past lovers in one cove, and a single man smoking a cigarette in another. His eyes narrow, follow my every step. The smoke curls up as he watches me.

As the light starts to fade, and the clouds grow a deeper pink, I start taking pictures of the Temple of Apollo. A crescent moon and the first star of the evening are behind it. I click pictures from every angle. The sky grows darker. The light changes on the broken columns.

When it is too dark for more pictures I begin to walk out of the wooded shore toward the boat. Two dogs bark at me from behind the bushes. They run toward me, teeth bared. One nudges my hips and then my hand. They keep pushing against me, and jumping up. They don't growl. Then the darker one sinks his teeth into the base of my thumb. I pull my hands away, raise them over my head and call out for help.

A man on a bicycle says, "I think I can distract them." He whistles. The dogs turn around and follow him for half a block. I walk away as fast as I can. The dogs turn again and come toward me. They trot beside me back to the boat, nudge my hips with their noses. I keep my arms folded in front of me.

When I get back on the boat I look for Norm, but he's not back yet. I show my bloody wound to the guide. "Wash it with disinfectant soap and put a medication on it," he says.

"It's swelling," I say.

"Don't worry. We don't have rabies on this island. I think you will be all right," he says.

When Norm returns I show him my hand. "What happened?" he asks. I look at him, shrug my shoulders, say, "Oh, it's nothing," and toss back to him the last of the pistachios.

Road Construction

She stands beside the highway,
dressed in her burgundy sari,
lifting the sledgehammer,
breaking black rocks
into smaller ones.
A goat grazes on the stubble
of cut sugar cane near her baby
who lies sleeping
in a trench close by the road.
He lies on a small blanket.
Another small blanket covers him.
He breathes the diesel fumes
from trucks and busses
passing to and from Aurangabad.

The woman scoops the rocks
onto a round cupped tray
which she places on her head,
then walks a few yards,
bends forward, and empties
the rocks into the trench
where a man is pouring asphalt
from a bucket.

Another man sleeps in the trench
a half-block down the road
from the sleeping baby.
There is no blanket under him
or over him.

The baby must be a boy.
She would have killed an infant daughter
like the other women do.
Soon she will cripple this baby,
like the other women do,
to make him a successful beggar.

Push Back

Put the band-aid
on the spot
where the foot padding
is so thin
the skin blisters and bruises.
Find thick, absorbent socks,
and shoes wide enough
so the bunion doesn't hurt.
Stretch for twenty minutes
so the lumbar radiculitis doesn't flare up.
Change from 2 lb. to 3 lb. weights
for the upper arms.
Lift weights on the ankles
for the upper thigh.
Walk four miles a day
instead of three,
more aerobics for the heart.

Pretend you remember
what you went after
when you walked from
one room to another.
Pretend the glasses are not
getting stronger every year.
Pretend you don't need
to pee every hour.

Push before arthritis wracks the joints.
Push before senility dulls the brain.
Push before diabetes blinds the eye.
Push before hearing fades to silence.
Push before stroke slurs the speech.
Push before heart attack explodes the chest.
Push before cancer shreds the gut.

Keep up the illusion of control.

Between Breaths

Hand in hand,
the fingers interlaced,
shoulders bumping,
she walks with him.
The outer hands hold the leather leashes
as the dogs pull ahead,
then stop to pee and sniff the air.
They talk of what to broil for dinner,
chicken or fish?
They talk of tonight's workout at the gym,
weights or aerobics, or both?
They talk about the day, the irritating call,
the speech to give tomorrow.
He tells her a joke to put in the speech.

He doesn't see it coming,
the car over the curb
on him, over him, crushing him,
crushing one dog,
knocking her out.
She wakes up.
The car is 80 yards away.
His crushed body is 80 yards away.
Between one breath and the next,
between one step and another,
everything changes forever.

This breath,
moves in, moves out.
So it was in the moments after my birth.
So it will be in the moments before my death,
and again in the next birth
if there is a next birth.
But the breath,

inhaled by the tiger in Chitwan Park in Nepal,
the rat that ran past my door last night,
the dolphin as he dances
in and out of the water off Maui,
the lion as he eats his breakfast of zebra
in the dawn sunlight on the Masai Mara,
this breath is the all in the all,
the shared oxygen and nitrogen
between me and the all of all.
After the moment of my last breath
the breath will go on,
inhaled by all the others:
my children,
the philodendron,
the ladybug on the leaf,

When the man had
all the breath knocked out of him
by the car that took his life,
his last breath went out
into the surrounding air,
into the grass, the palm trees,
the surviving dog,
into her, and his life goes on.

Angel

This week,
when bombs fell
and refugees trudged
miles through cold
to find a place
to lay their heads;
this week,
as students shot rifles
and threw bombs at their school;
this week,
on an ordinary Thursday,
I fell on a raised inch of sidewalk.
My chin split
and my blood flowed.

A stranger stepped up,
told me where to press
to stop the blood,
stayed with me
until I called for help,
until my husband came
to drive me to the hospital.
The man said he was a student
and an off-duty cop.
I was grateful.
Of all the world in need of angels
he found me here in mine,
and brought with him
just what I needed,
ice and towels,
and a chance to forget
everything else.

Security

Last year, in Quito, Ecuador, we walked down a narrow street, past pretty, landscaped homes. Each was surrounded by high garden walls with shards of broken glass embedded on top. Some had coils of barbed wire on the glass. Through one gate we saw a modern house, a lot like ours at home. A German shepherd barked from the rooftop as we passed. A shopkeeper told us, "Thieves stand on cars, throw old mattresses over the glass and barbed wire on the walls, and hoist themselves across the top. They risk their lives to steal what they can."

At noon today in Los Angeles we drive home from a bike ride at the ocean. As we turn into the driveway, a security guard in front of our house motions for us to reverse the car. I roll down a window.

"What's going on?" I ask.

"Your house has been broken into," he answers. "Wait for the police to get here. Someone might still be inside."

We watch as four policemen with guns drawn enter the house. Five minutes later they come out, no burglar in sight. "You can go in now," one says. Two security guards join us as we enter.

Shattered glass and pieces of a garden pot litter the kitchen floor. Blood spots stain the counter. We walk through the house to our bedroom where my jewelry is scattered across the bed. "Don't touch it," The policeman says. I lean over, study the mess closely. My diamond engagement ring, three other gold rings, and gold watch are missing. Silver necklaces and glass beads are still here. Norm's wallet and two gold rings sit on his desk where he left them. I wonder why the thief took my jewelry and not Norm's.

We walk through each room, find everything else as we left it, except for a bloody towel near the front door.

The security guard says, "I was at your house one minute after the alarm went off. The thief must have known how long it would take from the first ring of the alarm until we'd get to your house. Is someone mad at you? It looks like it was done by someone who knows your house."

"No one I can think of," I answer.

As soon as everyone leaves our house, I pull out the phone book to look up the numbers of window repair services, companies that sell guard dogs, and contractors who build high garden walls.

Hands

I notice my hands in the mirror.
Veins splayed across the surface,
bumpy ridges like the roots
of a banyan tree.
Skin with lines as though
a family of spiders have been
weaving intricate webs.
These hands have
reined in horses,
steered cars across the Rockies,
diapered babies,
caressed lovers,
cooked and cleaned up
from countless meals,
pulled on snow-suits and galoshes,
photographed lions,
edited video,
painted, gardened,
played piano,
shoveled mounds of high white snow,
scooped soil into parents' graves.

Now, as they lift my grandson,
I pray they stay strong enough.

Almost Flying

The Wingless Cormorant,
perched on a rock
on the Galapagos Islands,
flaps his vestigial wings,
expecting to fly
like his ancestors did,
before evolution grounded them.
Eventually he hops and rolls
off the rock
to capture the worm
of his desire.

Joshua, five months old,
in Kirksville, Missouri,
spots a toy
three feet in front of him
on the carpet.
He flaps his arms and legs.
His heavy belly
keeps him grounded
like the Cormorant
He drops his head down,
pulls up his legs,
and rolls past the toy,
forgets it,
and begins to study
his reflection
in a mirror.

This boy will fly.

Three Ropes of Challa Dough

When my daughter, Lisa, was three days old
I went to the kitchen to bake challa.
I wanted something rising again in the oven.
I sifted flour, salt, and sugar,
started the yeast in warm water,
mixed the eggs, oil, and yeast
in the center of the flour,
kneaded it all
until it came alive in my hands,
let it rise,
then rolled three ropes of dough
to braid into challa
for Sabbath dinner.
It rose with its own life inside
from the life-giving yeast.
I baked the bread
until it was crusty and golden
on the outside,
soft and delicious on the inside.

Like my granddaughter, Miriam,
tough and sweet,
with intertwining strengths:
her Chinese birth parents,
her Jewish and Christian adoptive parents,
her own life force, all of it,
mixed and kneaded, rising like bread dough,
growing to become an American woman
for the new Millennium.

Hineni—Here I Am

Joshua calls, *Grandma Jean, where are you?*
Here I am I answer. *Where are you?*
I here, he calls back. *I Josh.*

I learn from him about the mystery
of God and our prayers.
God calls, *Abraham!*
Hineni—Here I am, Abraham answers,
totally present,
ready to respond and obey,
as I am when Joshua calls.

Grandma Jean, sit down right there,
Joshua commands.
I sit down.
I play with animals, he announces.
He picks up a toy lion
and places it on the table,
then a tiger and a giraffe.

Shema Yisroael, God tells us.
Listen up, you people.
Adonai Elohenu.
I am The Lord.
Adonai ehod. And I am one.
Pay attention. I am everything
and I am One.

I reach to move the lion
to the other side of the table.
No, says Joshua.
Lion right there!
I listen, I hear,
and I draw my hand back.

Breakfast News

Miriam kneels on her chair
at the breakfast table.
She doesn't want
the high chair any more,
but can't reach the table
from the kitchen chair.
She eats a bowl of Cheerios and milk
with a spoon and doesn't spill a drop.
She drinks juice from her sipping cup.
"Your Mommy used to eat
  cereal with her fingers
  when she was a baby," I tell her.
She puts down her spoon
  and looks at me.
  I sip my coffee.
"Grandma Jean," she says,
"you didn't know me
  when I was a baby."
"You're right, I didn't," I answer.
"My Mommy went
  to China to get me."
  I nod, catch my breath,
  and take a bite of toast.
"Are you going with my Mommy
  to get my baby sister?" she asks.
  I nod again. "Yes, I'll go with her.
  We'll be leaving pretty soon," I say.
  She sips some juice.
"Will you wait for us at home?" I ask.
  Now Miriam nods,
  picks up her spoon,
  and continues to eat her Cheerios,
  one spoonful at a time,
  spilling nothing.

From the Window

In an air conditioned,
sightseeing tour bus
I look out on the streets
of Hefei, China.
We have just passed a refrigerator factory
and crowded five-story apartment buildings,
where laundry hangs from every balcony.
Three bird cages with canaries
hang beside the laundry of one apartment.
Potted plants grow behind the railings.
In the distance I spot a nuclear reactor.
Now we pass a row of three-story,
single family houses
beside a lake where ducks glide and lotus bloom.
Koi swim under the surface.
Shiny new cars stand in the driveways.

In my arms rides baby Huai Xiu Xia
soon to become my American granddaughter, Rose.
Beside the bus, a man pedals a three-wheeled cart
loaded with bales of rice piled high as his head.
Sitting on top rides his grandmother.
She looks through the window
at Rose, then at me. Our eyes meet.
Rose reaches for my glasses,
pokes her fingers in my mouth,
blows bubbles as I croon to her.

Walking Home

We, American parents and grandparents,
walk home through crowded streets in Guangzhou.
Our adopted babies ride on our bodies in slings.
Girls, six to ten years old,
press roses into our hands,
and beg for yuan in return.
We cross our arms, shake our heads,
say *no, no, no,* but they persist,
and lay roses on the sleepy infants.
We return the roses, say *No thank you.*
Suddenly one of the girls
drops to her knees, wailing *ai, ai, ai.*
A taxi door has hit her as it opened.
We can't tell if she is truly hurt,
maybe a broken rib.
Other young girls surround her.
No Chinese mother approaches.
The local passengers
get out of their cab
and walk off.
The cab driver pulls away.
The girl wails louder.
We look at each other, shake our heads,
and walk on to the hotel with our babies.
One of us still has a rose on her sling.

One Poet's Beginning

Rose toddles around the room,
pulls a xylophone off the shelf,
and bangs it with a mallet.
I pull the string of a dog on wheels,
"Doggie, doggie," I say.
Rose says, "Og."
She picks up a stacking cup
and puts in into a larger cup.
"Cup," I say.
She looks at me,
then pulls a book
off the shelf.
She points to a dog picture,
and says, "Og."
She stands up,
turns herself around,
pushes her tush into my lap,
points to the dog again.
"Og," she says,
I take the book
and turn the pages in front of her.
"Bee. . . bzz," and "ball," I say.
"Og," she says,
and giggles.

The Touch

Outside the airport I pace
and watch for the green van
coming to pick us up.
It pulls over to the curb.
I throw my suitcases into the hatch
and climb in the back seat.
My husband gets in front
beside our daughter-in-law.
Our grandson, Joshua, sleeps in his car seat.
We drive 60 miles to their home.
I hear Josh's soft snore.
Then he stretches, opens his eyes,
and looks around.
He sees Norm in front
and me in back beside him.
"Grandma," he says, "are you an airplane?"
"No, Josh," I answer.
"I got off the airplane
while you were asleep.
Now I'm riding with you and Grandpa
in your Mommy's car.
We're going to your house."
He reaches a hand toward me.
I reach toward him.
He takes hold of my finger.
Thirty minutes later he's still touching it.

I think of the painting by Michelangelo
on the ceiling of the Sistine Chapel:
God reaching out,
and Adam reaching up.

Sighting Liberty

We stand in a line six deep and two blocks long.
Jugglers toss their tenpins to entertain us.
Ghanan men sell Rolex watches
from their leather brief cases.
People around me speak French,
Japanese, German, Swedish, Farsi.
A fog horn sounds.
The ferry docks at Battery Park.
We run up the gangplank,
climb to the top deck
for the best view of Lady Liberty.
The boat circles around Ellis Island
until the Statue comes into sight.
I don't expect to be impressed.

There she is, arm raised, with the torch in hand,
wide blank eyes, flowing skirts.
Suddenly I'm sobbing.
Grandma comes into my mind,
how she must have looked at 25,
holding my mother, two years old, by one hand,
and four-year-old Anna, by the other.
Grandma had climbed out to the deck from her bunk,
where she lay for most of the trip,
exhausted from alternate seasickness and hunger.
She had eaten only salt herring
all the way from Russia,
not to sin by eating food that was not kosher.
She looks at the statue,
points it out to her little girls, and looks around.
She knows that Grandpa won't meet her on the shore.
She reaches inside her blouse to touch
his letter and the train ticket to Wisconsin.
Soon she will have to gather her trunk, comforters,

pillows, candlesticks, and daughters.
Speaking no English,
she will have to clear Ellis Island immigration,
find the right train,
and cross half of America
with the last of her salt herring.

She spits out the taste of salt and bile,
sighs, pulls Anna and Sarah
away from the railing,
and returns to her crumpled bunk.

My Muzzle

My grandmother used to say,
"Nye hei budgeh yak Soreh kazala."
How to translate this?
     Whatever you say.
     Don't make waves.
     Don't speak your mind.

Grandma always chose peace
over standing her ground.
She had her reasons.
Grandma's mother raged
at the daughter who spoke her mind.
In their village, near Minsk,
those who spoke out were taken.
She survived the pogroms,
hiding under the floor boards
or up in the barn.
When she got to America she did
like the others on Ellis Island,
those who stifled their coughs,
hid their blemishes,
and didn't speak their minds
for fear of being sent back.

So this is what Grandma taught me:
"Nye hei budgeh yak Soreh kazala."
     Don't say what you think,
     or who you are,
     or what you've done.

I was a good girl.
I hid my blemishes,
I stifled my coughs,
I hid the truth until I was 15,
when I realized that I wasn't like Grandma.
I wanted to stand up for the truth.

Now I'm not so sure anyone
knows what's right, or what's true.
I have so little time left,
and I don't know how to spend it.
Should I go upstairs or down?
Should I return phone calls
or clean the closet?
Should I write poems and stories,
or not?

I was 50 before I found out that
Great Aunt Eva had a nervous breakdown,
Great Aunt Sarah had a lover,
Cousin Hymie drank too much.
When I start to write
my muzzle reminds me to question:
What can I tell?
What should I keep hidden?
What must I leave out?

"Nye hei budgeh yak Sorah kazala."
          Hide the truth,
Grandma still admonishes.

Taboos

This pen
moves across the empty page.
This poet
hurls words against the gods,
words to change the world,
inner, outer,
words to break the old taboos,
words to shake the future
into new forms.

She forgets.
The taboos have lasted longer
than her scribbling.
The tribe gathered its wisdom
for centuries and millennia.
Who does she think she is
to speak unkind truths
about the dead?
Who does she think she is
to crack the secret doors
meant to stay shut?

Raphael Patai writes about
two cherubim in "marital embrace"
in the great temple of Jerusalem
in the center of the center,
in the Holy of Holies.
Look what happened when
the people looked at that mystery!
It is two thousand years later
and they are still weeping
by that broken old wall.

Beware of breaking the taboos!
Only the gods know
what they may unleash.

Dawn

I try to remember the morning prayers
Grandpa never taught me
because I was a girl.
Every morning at dawn
he stood at the eastern wall of our house,
wrapped in his white and black prayer shawl,
leather straps around his hairy arms,
black wooden box on his forehead,
black skullcap on his head.
He swayed and chanted,
praising God who restored him to life,
who made him a Jew,
who did not make him a woman,
who returned light to the world every morning.
It seemed to me then that
light increased in the room
with every chant.
I remember old men in Jerusalem,
wrapped in their prayer shawls,
hurrying to the synagogue at dawn
to welcome the day with the other men.
I remember men and women
at the edge of the Ganges River
in Veranasi, India.
They bowed and swayed,
chanted prayers,
lit candles on leaves and
floated them into the filthy, sacred river
just as the sun rose over the water.
Some jumped into the river to bathe
with the ashes of corpses
at the exact moment of sunrise.
In Hong Kong I saw men and women
do their slow tai chi ballet in the parks

as as others were driving to work
on the crowded roads.
In Los Angeles the street lights
are still on as I step outside,
inhale the crisp air.
I see a few stars and the moon
even though there is light across the sky,
different from the darkness of night,
blue gray above,
pale yellow at the horizon.
The clouds change color as I walk.
Stripes of pink fade to purple
to the north, orange to the south.
Sycamores have dropped their leaves,
and chains of seed pods
hang from their branches.
The first camellias of winter
are just starting to open.
I don't really know how to pray
yet I bless the growing light,
praise the Source of light,
and say how grateful I am
that I can see it.

Messenger

On Saturday I spot a fox
on my neighbor's garage roof.
Cars roar down my street.
Dogs bark.
An ambulance siren screams.
The fox looks at me.
I stare back,
blink, look again,
point out the fox
for a passing jogger.
The fox turns,
disappears beside the roof.

Later that morning,
in the synagogue,
I sing familiar melodies,
chant the prayers.
Listen to the rabbi speak
about modern and ancient ideas:
James Hillman and Rashi,
Freud and Reb Nachman of Bratzlav,
Philip Roth and Isaac Luria of Tsfat.
He suggests that we experiment
with keeping the Sabbath.

When I was a child
In Grandpa's house
I tried to sneak around the rules.
Sabbath was a day of
Don't do anything fun,
not of *peace and joy.*
Now I don't turn on the computer,
make phone calls,
or run to the store,

until the first three stars shine.
I sing the prayers,
greet and hug friends,
eat a delicious lunch,
and spend the afternoon reading poetry.

I think of the fox again.
He must have been
my Sabbath messenger,
a sly reminder to be grateful
for the gift of Sabbath.

Tillandsia Cyanea

Every Thursday I water it
The leaves arch and point like field grass.
The flower, green on the sides
and pink in the center,
shaped like a canoe paddle,
has overlapping scales on both sides,
like rhythm,
like music.
Every third day a three-petaled purple blossom
bursts out between one scale and the next,
just as the previous one fades,
first on the right side,
then on the left,
always moving up,
until the last emerges,
a tune moving up the scale
reaching the top and fading.

I can't rush this blooming.
I can't delay it.
"Just water it," I tell myself,
"Just water it,
just look,
and listen."

Pruning

At my house
I haul out
piles of old magazines,
journals, files,
things we haven't used in years,
old clothes, shoes, dishes.
I've even given eight grocery bags
full of books to the library book sale.
I've erased names
in my telephone Rolodex,
and started one more diet.

When I walk back
from the trash
I look at the tree
at my neighbor's house.
We thought it was dead.
Every February it used to bloom
in a wide yellow canopy
over the driveway,
but nothing has bloomed
for the past three years.
A few months ago
the neighbors had the tree pruned,
so that, now, with all
the old dead wood cut away,
one branch is sprouting
as though it thinks
it's a whole young tree.
I study the reborn tree every day,
call it my teacher,
learning what I can
from the buds of yellow blossoms,
hanging from the one remaining branch
of the tree we thought was dead.

Invasion

My roses and geraniums bloom
bright as yesterday.
The refrigerator is stocked with melons.
A plague of locust threatens somewhere,
yet I look out my window
at a clear blue sky.
My nephew phones to tell us
the stock market is up.
"It may be the bounce
of a dead cat," he says.
What can I make of all this—
ordinary gifts of ordinary days,
and the persistent clamor
of plagues beyond?
I focus on the computer screen
in front of me
and type a few more syllables.

We Persist

This speech we write,
its source mysterious as birth,
its womb sprung
strong and wild,
or limp and frail;
this speech we write
into the echoing air,
or on the page,
is heard as the ear distorts it.
The brain,
ringing with constant chatter,
takes in a little,
scrambles it up like eggs,
until what passes for conversation
is the aphasic babble
of human shells,
attentive, wise, and proud
in photographs,
yet deaf to each other's epic nonsense.
Silly women and men.
We persist, in spite of everything,
until, at last, it doesn't matter,
and still we persist,
wrapped in afghans,
pushed from TV set to table,
and then to bed,
the scent of urine in the halls,
where the children come to visit,
and start another round.

Clutter

I dread the mail,
the time it takes,
piles of envelopes to toss,
contribution requests to grant or deny,
and magazines I have no time to read.
My office overflows with bulletins,
flyers from restaurants,
newspaper clippings,
recipes, notebooks,
catalogues for clothes I plan to order,
books of bargain coupons.
I tell you, this clutter that I can not outrace,
that grows and grows without ceasing,
oppresses me so much
that I can hardly do anything.
My To Do list
grows faster than the clutter.

I see myself in a plain pine box one day.
No satin lining for me,
no pillow, no handles.
just a cushion made of all the poems
I never revised,
letters I never answered,
clippings I never sent to friends,
my body on a mess of my own making.
As they lower me I'll still be clutching
the last article I wanted to read.

The Promise

*"I will make My covenant with you, and all life will
never be cut short by the waters of a flood. There
will never again be a flood to destroy the earth."
God said, "This is the sign that I am providing for
the covenant between Me, you, and every living
creature that is with you, for everlasting
generations: I have placed My rainbow in the
clouds, and it shall be a sign of the covenant
between Me and the earth."*
Genesis 9:8-9:17

It's afternoon, December 31, 2000.
In the kitchen I arrange raw vegetables
into a pattern of red peppers,
cauliflower, carrots, squash, radishes,
jicama, celery, cherry tomatoes.
I hear Richard Stoltzman play
New York Counterpoint on the radio.
An announcer interrupts,
"The Year 2000 just came to Australia.
No Y2K breakdowns reported.
No airline difficulties."
I shrug, sigh, and cut the cucumbers.
I must admit that this morning
I went out to buy more bottled water
and canned fruit and soup.
Outside it's been raining.
Now, through the window,
I see a rainbow,
intense bands of purple, red,
orange, yellow, green, and blue,
I open the door for a better view
of the great arc
across the tree tops.
God seems to be keeping
the promise so far.

The Other Side

When my friend's sister died
she appeared to be fighting with someone.
She seemed to be telling them,
"I won't go with you. I don't want to."
Finally she relaxed and passed over,
as though the right guide had come at last.
Who will come for me, I wonder?
My mother or my father?
When it was time to visit Daddy after their divorce
I'd walk four blocks down the street
from our house to Dad's rented room.
My stomach ache got worse with every step.
I imagine that when I die
Mother will be reaching for me, waiting for me,
just like she did every day
when I came home from school.
wanting to know every detail
of where I went, with whom I spoke,
what I did, especially what I ate.
She'll follow me into the bathroom.
She'll sit right next to the telephone
so she can hear every word if a friend happens to call.
She'll hover over me as I cook,
commenting on the health hazards
of every ingredient I use.
I don't want to go with her either.
I imagine that when I die,
Mother will tell me how bad I have been
for telling all the family secrets in my poems.
"Never tell people your personal business,"
was the rule of the family.
I've broken that rule, and so many others.
They may not even want me on the other side.
Who will come for me, then, if not them?
Maybe I'll tell them I'm waiting for someone else.

Counting Backwards

Let's see,
if I have to be there at 5:15,
I should leave here at 4:15,
so I must stop and dress by 3:15,
and, before that,
I need to pick up my dress
at the cleaners,
so I can only do one more project.

That's how I lead my life,
counting backwards.

Let's see,
with a little luck I may live till 91,
so I should buy the plot by 90,
clean out everything
I want to give away by 85,
write 5 books by 80,
read all the great writers and poets by 70.

Meanwhile, I've got to
walk 4 miles every day,
water the plants,
hug Norm 12 times a day,
cook breakfast and dinner,
answer the mail,
throw out the catalogues,
pay the bills,
go to work.
Only 6 years left
to read the great books.

I add a line to the bottom
of my To Do list:
Live to 97.

Young As Ever

It's time to grow a soul,
deeper than the creases on my face.

A friend says,
"As the creases deepen
the vision blurs,
so we stay
as young as ever,"

but young as ever
is not my goal.

The years are writing
poems on my face.

Afterword

My mother's voice echoes in my poems. Sarah Kohler Yager read nursery rhymes to me. I memorized and recited them on my father's early morning radio program. Even when she could no longer remember her grandchildren's names she remembered the poems she had written as a young woman. My father, Jack Yager, spoke English, Polish, Yiddish, Russian, Hebrew, German, and Spanish. I can still hear his voice over the radio on a country music program heard by all the farmers in Iowa, his Yiddish accent extolling the virtues of work shirts and overalls from his store. In my teen years I heard my grandparent's Yiddish spoken at home and English spoken with German and Swedish accents on the streets of my home town in Wisconsin. My grandmother, who spoke broken English and read and wrote only Yiddish, would pick unusual English phrases off the radio and repeat them as she walked around the house. When she kneaded bread or washed laundry on a scrub board she quoted Yiddish and Russian parables. When a baseball game came on the radio she would call out "Bombers banditen varfen a pilke und me schreit Ray Ray Syracuse" (Bums and bandits throw a ball and then everyone cheers Hooray for Syracuse). Every day I heard my grandpa chant the Hebrew morning and evening prayers. In high school, Mrs. Lahti, a speech teacher, encouraged me to perform lines from Shakespeare, Shaw, and Yeats.

Some poets influenced me through personal contact. Marcia Cohn Spiegel invited me to join The Creative

Jewish Women's Alliance, and introduced me to her collection of Jewish women's poetry spanning 2000 years. My friends in the CJWA have supported my growth as a writer. Deena Metzger helped me use the writing process to open painful memories. When those memories were exposed to light and air they could dissipate, though never disappear. Jack Grapes taught me to recognize and use a variety of voices found in contemporary poetry. My classmates in Deena's and Jack's writing and editing classes have inspired me with their courage, gifts, skill, and caring feedback.

When Jim Shaw took my poems into juvenile detention camps where he interviewed children who had committed murder, some of those wounded children wrote poems for him. This helped me see my own work in a new light.

In reading the poems of Sharon Olds I learned that it is possible to transform the most painful childhood experiences into art. From May Sarton I learned to really see a drop of water or a mote of dust floating in a sun ray. She also taught me to welcome the mature years of life. Adrienne Rich gave me an expanded language for anger at injustice in this world. From Richard Jones I have learned the elegance of simplicity. Annie Dillard taught me to recognize the power of a single moment.

All these voices and more have fed my ability to tap into my experiences and transform them into poems. For all of these voices, for their being, for their art I am profoundly grateful.

And for Alan Berman's meticulous editing and formatting of *Chaos and Dancing Stars* I am appreciative beyond words.